Is it...?

slippery or sticky

Vic Parker

Heinemann
LIBRARY

Little Nippers

www.heinemann.co.uk/library
Visit our website to find out more information about **Heinemann Library** books.

To order:
☎ Phone 44 (0) 1865 888066
🖷 Send a fax to 44 (0) 1865 314091
🖳 Visit the Heinemann Bookshop at www.heinemann.co.uk/library to browse our catalogue and order online.

First published in Great Britain by Heinemann Library, Halley Court, Jordan Hill, Oxford OX2 8EJ, part of Harcourt Education.
Heinemann is a registered trademark of Harcourt Education Ltd.

Editorial: Jilly Attwood and Claire Throp
Design: Jo Hinton-Malivoire and bigtop, Bicester, UK
Models made by: Jo Brooker
Picture Research: Rosie Garai and Sally Smith
Production: Séverine Ribierre

Originated by Dot Gradations
Printed and bound in China by South China Printing Company

ISBN 0 431 17403 2 (hardback)
08 07 06 05 04
10 9 8 7 6 5 4 3 2 1

ISBN 0 431 17408 3 (paperback)
08 07 06 05 04
10 9 8 7 6 5 4 3 2 1

British Library Cataloguing in Publication Data
Parker, Vic
Is it slippery or sticky?
620.1'1292
A full catalogue record for this book is available from the British Library.

Acknowledgements
The publishers would like to thank Gareth Boden for permission to reproduce photographs.

Cover photograph reproduced with permission of Gareth Boden.

The publishers would like to thank Annie Davy for her assistance in the preparation of this book.

Every effort has been made to contact copyright holders of any material reproduced in this book. Any omissions will be rectified in subsequent printings if notice is given to the publishers.

The paper used to print this book comes from sustainable resources.

2

Contents

Time for a treasure hunt

This teacher wants to make a display of **sticky** and slippery things.

4

What can the children find at home?

Search for something slippery

What a sloppy, slippery mess!

6

A plastic apron is slippery, so it's easy-peasy to wipe clean.

Spot something sticky

sticky doughnuts

sticky mouth and fingers

9

Whee! A slippy slide is too **big** for our collection.

10

But small **sticky** buds are just right!

Slippery soap

Wet soap.
Slimy water.
Super slippy...

whooops!

13

Sticky plaster.
There, there ...

15

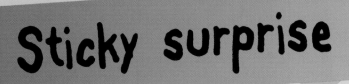

Sticky surprise

It's someone's birthday!

16

Can you spot **sticky** things for the display?

Here comes the sun

In the summer, slap on some **slippery** sun lotion ...

and slurp on a sticky ice-pop.

A hair-raising find

sticky

21

Classroom display

sticky things

Index

The end

Notes for adults

The *Is it . . .?* series provides young children with a first opportunity to examine and learn about common materials. The books follow a boy and girl as they go on a treasure hunt around their house to find items with contrasting textures. There are four titles in the series and when used together, the books will encourage children to express their curiosity and explore their environment. The following Early Learning Goals are relevant to this series:

Creative development
Early learning goals for exploring media and materials:
• explore colour, texture, shape, form and space in two or three dimensions
• begin to describe the texture of things.

Knowledge and understanding of the world
Early learning goals for exploration and investigation:
• investigate objects and materials by using all of their senses as appropriate
• show curiosity, observe and manipulate objects
• describe simple features of objects
• look closely at similarities, differences, patterns and change.

This book introduces the reader to a range of everyday items that are slippery or sticky. It will extend young children's thinking about familiar objects and enable them to talk expressively about different materials. The book will help children extend their vocabulary, as they will hear new words such as *display* and *slimy*. You may like to introduce and explain other new words yourself, such as *surface* and *texture*.

Follow-up activities
• Help your child improve their number ability by asking them to find ten slippery things and ten sticky things around the house.
• Fill some bowls with slippery foods, such as peeled, sliced mango, wet, fresh fish, tinned spaghetti. Then fill some bowls with sticky foods, such as jam, cookie mixture, honey. Play a guessing game by blindfolding the children and telling them to dip their hand into each bowl, to identify the contents. (Depending on the contents of the bowls, they could taste the foods too, to help them guess.)